Digital Marketing 001 (Dummies Guide)

TABLE OF CONTENT

I0422127

- Encouragement for Continued Growth

- Final Thoughts and Best Wishes on Your Digital Marketing Journey

Welcome and Brief Overview

Welcome to the Exciting World of Digital Marketing!

Congratulations on taking your first steps into the dynamic realm of digital marketing! Whether you're a curious newcomer or a business enthusiast seeking to expand your skills, this journey promises to be both thrilling and rewarding.

Overview: What is Digital Marketing?

Picture this: You're standing at the crossroads of technology and creativity, with a vibrant landscape of possibilities unfolding before you. That's the essence of digital marketing – a powerful blend of art and science that leverages digital channels to connect businesses with their audience.

In simpler terms, digital marketing is the art of reaching people where they are: online. It's about crafting compelling stories, creating visually captivating content, and using strategic techniques to grab the attention of potential customers in the vast digital space.

Why Digital Marketing Matters

Now, you might be wondering, "Why does digital marketing matter?" Well, in a world where everyone is online, from social media enthusiasts to avid blog readers and frequent shoppers, digital marketing becomes the bridge that connects businesses with their target audience. It's not just about showcasing products or services; it's about building relationships, sparking conversations, and creating memorable experiences.

Interactive Challenge: Explore Your Digital Presence

Let's make this interactive! Take a moment to think about your online interactions today. Did you scroll through social media? Read an article or blog? Maybe even make an online purchase? Congratulations, you've been part of the digital landscape!

Activity: Share your last online interaction in the comments below. It could be a favorite Instagram post, an interesting blog you read, or a product you recently discovered online.

Remember, every click, like, and share you make is a part of the vast digital ecosystem, and as a digital marketer, you'll learn to navigate and influence this landscape to achieve your goals.

What's Next?

In the upcoming chapters, we'll delve into the exciting realms of social media marketing, search engine optimization, content creation, and much more. Each section will equip you with practical skills and insights, making the world of digital marketing not just accessible but also enjoyable.

Get ready to unleash your creativity, dive into analytics, and embark on a journey where every click is a new opportunity. Welcome to the fascinating universe of digital marketing, where the possibilities are as limitless as your imagination!

The Digital Revolution: Importance of Digital Marketing in Today's Business Landscape

Introduction: Unveiling the Digital Era

Welcome to the age of digital transformation! In this chapter, we'll delve into why digital marketing has become the cornerstone of success in today's business landscape. Get ready to embark on a journey that will revolutionize the way you perceive marketing.

1. The Shift from Traditional to Digital:

- Explore the evolution from traditional marketing methods to the digital realm.

- Understand how consumer behavior has changed with the rise of digital channels.

2. Global Reach and Accessibility:

- Unleash the power of the internet in breaking down geographical barriers.

- Learn how digital marketing opens doors to a global audience for businesses of all sizes.

3. Cost-Effectiveness and ROI:

- Delve into the cost advantages of digital marketing over traditional advertising.

- Grasp the concept of return on investment (ROI) and how it plays a pivotal role.

4. Interactivity and Engagement:

- Discover the interactive nature of digital marketing.

- Learn how to engage your audience through social media, emails, and other digital channels.

Interactive Segment: "Digital Vs. Traditional Quiz"

Test your knowledge on the differences between traditional and digital marketing with our fun quiz!

5. Real-Time Analytics and Insights:

- Unlock the world of real-time data analytics.

- See how data-driven decisions can transform your marketing strategies.

6. Targeted Marketing:

- Dive into the art of precision with targeted marketing.

- Understand how digital platforms allow you to tailor messages for specific audiences.

Interactive Segment: "Create Your First Targeted Ad"

Put your knowledge to the test by crafting a targeted ad for a hypothetical product. We'll guide you through the process step by step.

7. Building Brand Credibility:

- Explore how digital marketing contributes to brand credibility.

- Learn the importance of online reviews, testimonials, and

social proof.

Interactive Segment: "Brand Building Challenge"

Share your thoughts on how you would build a brand's credibility in a digital world. Engage with other readers and gain valuable insights.

8. Adaptability to Trends and Changes:

- Uncover the agility of digital marketing in adapting to industry trends.

- Stay ahead by understanding the importance of continuous learning.

Interactive Segment: "Spot the Trend"

Test your trend-spotting skills with our interactive activity. Identify the latest digital marketing trends and discuss with fellow readers.

Conclusion: Embracing the Digital Frontier

As we wrap up this chapter, you now have a solid foundation on why digital marketing is not just a tool but a necessity in the modern business landscape. Get ready to explore the exciting digital marketing landscape in the upcoming chapters!

CHAPTER 1: UNDERSTANDING DIGITAL MARKETING

Section 1.1: What is Digital Marketing?

In the world of business and communication, digital marketing stands as a powerful force, shaping the way we connect with audiences and promote products or services. At its core, digital marketing involves leveraging digital channels, such as websites, social media, search engines, emails, and more, to reach potential customers. Unlike traditional marketing, which relies on physical media like print or television, digital marketing harnesses the vast potential of the online world.

Interactive Element: Digital Marketing Puzzle

Imagine digital marketing as a puzzle with various pieces representing different channels (social media, email, SEO, etc.). As you progress through the chapter, you'll gradually complete the puzzle, gaining a comprehensive view of how these pieces fit together.

Section 1.2: The Digital Landscape in a Nutshell

Picture the digital landscape as a vast, ever-expanding terrain with different touchpoints and platforms. Here's a quick summary:

Websites: The foundation of digital presence, like a storefront in the online world.

Social Media: Digital gatherings where people share, connect, and discover new things.

Search Engines: Gateways to information; users search, and businesses aim to be found.

Emails: Direct communication channels for personalized messages and updates.

Content: The fuel that powers the digital engine, providing value and information.

Interactive Element: Explore the Digital Landscape

An interactive map or diagram that allows beginners to click on each element and discover more about its role in digital marketing.

Section 1.3: The Power of Digital Marketing for Businesses

Digital marketing is not just a trend; it's a transformative force for businesses. Here's a snapshot:

Global Reach: Break geographical barriers and reach audiences worldwide.

Targeted Advertising: Pinpoint your audience based on demographics, interests, and behaviors.

Real-Time Interaction: Engage with your audience instantly, fostering relationships.

Measurable Results: Track and analyze campaigns, understanding what works and what doesn't.

Interactive Element: Business Simulation Game

Engage readers in a simulated scenario where they make decisions as a digital marketer for a fictional business. This helps to reinforce the practical application of digital marketing concepts.

Section 1.4: Key Concepts and Terminology

Digital marketing comes with its own set of terms and concepts. Here's a quick glossary:

SEO (Search Engine Optimization): Optimizing content to rank higher on search engine results.

CTR (Click-Through Rate): The percentage of people who click on an ad or link compared to the total number of viewers.

Engagement: Interactions and reactions from the audience, indicating interest.

Conversion: Desired actions taken by users, like making a purchase or filling out a form.

Interactive Element: Flashcards and Quizzes

Integrate flashcards or quizzes to help readers reinforce their understanding of key terms.

By the end of this chapter, readers should have a solid foundation in understanding what digital marketing is, its various components, and why it's a crucial aspect of modern business strategies.

Section 1: Definition and Scope of Digital Marketing

Interactive Element: Quiz

Question 1: What is digital marketing?

A. Traditional marketing

B. Online marketing

C. Both

Question 2: What is the primary goal of digital marketing?

A. Increase sales

B. Build brand awareness

C. Both

CHAPTER 2: DEVELOPING A STRONG FOUNDATION

In the ever-evolving landscape of digital marketing, building a robust foundation is the key to success. This chapter will guide you through the fundamental principles, ensuring you lay the groundwork for a prosperous journey in the digital marketing realm.

3. Understanding the Basics:

Digital Marketing 101: Explore the core concepts, terminologies, and the significance of digital marketing in today's business landscape.

-Channels Overview: Get a glimpse into the diverse channels available, including social media, SEO, content marketing, email, and paid advertising.

2. Building Your Marketing Knowledge:

Continuous Learning: Emphasize the importance of staying informed about industry trends, tools, and best practices.

Educational Resources: Explore beginner-friendly resources, courses, and communities where you can enhance your marketing knowledge.

3. Knowing Your Audience:

Importance of Targeting: Understand why knowing your audience is crucial and how it shapes your digital marketing strategy.

User Personas: Learn to create user personas to tailor your content and campaigns to specific demographics.

4. Setting Realistic Goals:

SMART Goals: Introduce the concept of SMART goals (Specific, Measurable, Achievable, Relevant, Time-bound) and how it applies to digital marketing.

Long-Term vs. Short-Term Objectives: Help readers distinguish between immediate wins and overarching goals.

Interactive Elements:

Self-Assessment Quizzes: Test your understanding of key concepts.

Case Studies: Explore real-world examples illustrating successful foundation-building strategies.

Workbook Exercises: Apply what you've learned through hands-on activities.

Summary:

Building a strong foundation in digital marketing is akin to constructing a sturdy building. Understand the basics, continuously learn, know your audience intimately, and set goals that propel you forward. This chapter equips you with the knowledge to navigate the vast digital landscape and sets the stage for your exciting journey into the world of digital marketing.

Key Takeaways:

1. Digital marketing involves a diverse set of channels and strategies.

2. Continuous learning is a cornerstone of success in digital marketing.

3. Knowing your audience and setting realistic goals are crucial for effective campaigns.

In the next chapter, we dive into the essential skills every digital marketer should possess, ensuring you're well-prepared for the challenges and opportunities that lie ahead.

Building Your Marketing Knowledge

In the fast-paced world of digital marketing, a solid foundation of marketing knowledge is crucial. This chapter is designed to guide beginners through the essentials, making learning interactive and easy to grasp.

1. Understanding the Basics:

   - Define marketing and its role in business.

   - Explore the four Ps of marketing (Product, Price, Place, Promotion).

   - Interactive Exercise: Create a simple marketing plan for a fictional product.

2. **Customer-Centric Approach:**

   - Emphasize the importance of understanding your target audience.

   - Explore buyer personas and how they inform marketing

strategies.

- Interactive Activity: Develop a customer persona for a chosen product or service.

3. Setting Realistic Goals:

- Discuss the significance of SMART goals (Specific, Measurable, Achievable, Relevant, Time-bound).

- Provide examples of short-term and long-term marketing objectives.

- Interactive Task: Outline personal marketing goals using the SMART framework.

4. Marketing Research:

- Introduce the basics of market research.

- Discuss tools and methods for gathering valuable market insights.

- Interactive Exercise: Conduct a simple market research survey or analysis.

5. Competitive Analysis:

- Explore the importance of understanding competitors.

- Provide templates for analyzing competitor strengths and weaknesses.

- Interactive Challenge: Analyze a competitor's digital presence and identify areas for improvement.

6. Marketing Mix in Digital Age:

- Adapt the traditional marketing mix to the digital landscape.

- Discuss the role of online channels in the product, price, place, and promotion strategies.

- Interactive Element: Create a digital marketing mix for a hypothetical product.

Building Your Marketing Knowledge in Digital Marketing

Introduction:

Digital marketing is a dynamic field that demands a solid foundation in marketing principles. In this chapter, we'll explore the essential knowledge areas that will set you on the path to becoming a successful digital marketer. Let's dive in!

3. Understanding Marketing Basics:

To succeed in digital marketing, you need a solid understanding of traditional marketing concepts. At its core, marketing is about identifying and satisfying customer needs. Learn about the 4 Ps (Product, Price, Place, Promotion) and how they shape marketing strategies.

Example: Consider how Apple's marketing focuses not just on the features of their products (Product) but also on creating a lifestyle (Promotion) associated with their brand.

2. Consumer Behavior:

Understanding your target audience is crucial. Dive into consumer behavior studies to comprehend what motivates people to make decisions.

Example: Analyze how companies like Amazon use personalized recommendations based on previous purchases to influence future buying decisions.

3. Market Research:

Learn the art of conducting market research to gather insights about your industry, competitors, and target audience. Utilize tools like surveys, interviews, and data analysis.

Example: Explore how Airbnb disrupted the hospitality industry by understanding the need for personalized travel experiences through extensive market research.

4. Segmentation, Targeting, Positioning (STP):

Segment your audience, select the most attractive segments, and position your product or service effectively. This strategic approach is fundamental in marketing.

Example: Coca-Cola successfully targets different segments with products like Diet Coke for health-conscious consumers and regular Coke for those seeking a classic taste.

5. Marketing Mix:

Understand how the combination of product, price, place, and promotion influences your marketing strategy. This knowledge helps in creating a cohesive and effective plan.

Example: Analyze how Starbucks combines a premium price strategy with a focus on creating a unique in-store experience (Place) and promoting seasonal offerings (Promotion).

6. Branding and Positioning:

A strong brand is a valuable asset. Learn how to build and manage a brand effectively, and understand the role of positioning in the minds of consumers.

Example: Nike's "Just Do It" campaign not only promotes products but also positions the brand as a symbol of motivation and empowerment.

7. Marketing Analytics:

In the digital age, data is king. Familiarize yourself with basic analytics tools and metrics to measure the success of your campaigns.

Example: Explore how Google Analytics helps businesses track website traffic, user behavior, and conversion rates for data-driven decision-making.

Real-Life Experience:

Early in my digital marketing journey, I delved into understanding consumer behavior and market research. I applied these insights to create targeted social media campaigns for a local startup. The engagement and conversion rates soared, showcasing the tangible impact of foundational marketing knowledge in the digital realm. Remember, every bit of knowledge you acquire is a stepping stone to becoming a proficient digital marketer. Stay curious and keep exploring!

Summary: Building Your Marketing Knowledge is like constructing a sturdy house start with a solid foundation. This chapter introduced you to the fundamental concepts of marketing, from the classic four Ps to the contemporary digital marketing mix. You discovered the importance of understanding your audience, setting achievable goals, conducting research, and staying aware of your competition.

Remember, marketing is both an art and a science. The interactive elements in this chapter are designed to help you apply what you've learned. As you move forward in your digital marketing journey, keep honing these foundational skills they will be your compass in the dynamic landscape of digital marketing. Now, let's put theory into practice!

Understanding the Target Audience in Digital Marketing

Introduction

Welcome to the exciting world of digital marketing! In this

chapter, we're going to dive into a crucial aspect of successful marketing – understanding your target audience. This knowledge forms the bedrock of effective digital campaigns, helping you connect with your audience on a personal level. Ready to unravel the mysteries of your potential customers? Let's get started!

1: Why Understanding Your Audience Matters

Personalization is Key: Explore the impact of personalized marketing on consumer engagement and brand loyalty.

Tailoring Your Message: Understand how audience insights allow you to craft messages that resonate with specific demographics.

2: Identifying Your Target Audience

Demographics: Learn to define your audience based on age, gender, location, income, and other key demographic factors.

Psychographics: Delve into the psychological aspects of your audience, understanding their interests, values, and lifestyles.

Interactive Exercise: Create Your Persona

Engage readers with an interactive persona-building exercise. Provide a template for creating a fictional representation of their ideal customer, including demographics, interests, and pain points.

Utilizing Data and Analytics:

Google Analytics: Introduce the basics of Google Analytics for tracking user behavior and demographics on websites.

Social Media Insights: Explore how platforms like Facebook and Instagram provide valuable data on audience engagement.

Interactive Insight: Analyzing Data

Include screenshots or step-by-step guides on interpreting data.

Encourage readers to explore their website analytics or social media insights.

Social Listening:

What is Social Listening: Define social listening and its role in understanding audience sentiments.

Tools and Techniques: Introduce beginner-friendly tools for social listening.

Interactive Activity: Social Listening Experiment

Encourage readers to conduct a simple social listening experiment. Provide a list of hashtags or keywords related to their industry and guide them on how to track conversations.

Summary:

Understanding your target audience involves more than just demographics; it's about comprehending the nuances of their behavior, interests, and desires. In this chapter, we covered the importance of personalization, how to identify your audience, leverage data and analytics, and the power of social listening. Armed with this knowledge, you're on your way to creating digital campaigns that truly resonate with your audience.

Remember, the more intimately you know your audience, the better you can tailor your marketing efforts to meet their needs and build lasting connections. Happy marketing!

Setting Realistic Goals and Objectives in Digital Marketing

Welcome to the exciting world of digital marketing! In this chapter, we'll guide you through the crucial process of setting realistic goals and objectives—a cornerstone for any successful digital marketing venture.

Understanding the Importance:

Why Set Goals?

Before diving into the digital marketing landscape, it's essential to have a roadmap. Goals serve as your guiding stars, helping you stay focused and measure your progress. They provide a clear direction, making your digital marketing efforts more purposeful.

Types of Goals in Digital Marketing

1. Awareness Goals

   - Introducing your brand to a broader audience.

   - Boosting visibility on social media platforms.

2. Engagement Goals

   - Increasing likes, shares, and comments on social media.

   - Enhancing interaction on your website or blog.

3. Conversion Goals

   - Turning website visitors into customers.

   - Encouraging sign-ups for newsletters or free trials.

4. Retention Goals

   - Building long-term relationships with existing customers.

   - Encouraging repeat business through loyalty programs.

SMART Criteria:

Specific

- Clearly define your goals. For instance, instead of "increase website traffic," specify "boost organic traffic by 20% in the next three months."

Measurable

- Establish concrete metrics to track your progress. Use tools like Google Analytics to quantify results.

Achievable

- Ensure your goals are realistic. Setting unattainable targets can lead to frustration and burnout.

Relevant

- Align your goals with your overall business objectives. Every digital marketing effort should contribute to the bigger picture.

Time-Bound

- Set deadlines for achieving your goals. This creates a sense of urgency and keeps you accountable.

Interactive Exercise: Define Your Goals

Let's make this interactive! Take a moment to jot down three digital marketing goals for your project or business. Share them in the comments or discuss them with a friend. Getting your goals down on paper is the first step toward turning your aspirations into achievements.

Insightful Tips

Start Small

- Begin with achievable goals. As you gain experience, you can aim higher.

Learn from Analytics

- Regularly analyze your data to understand what's working and what needs adjustment.

Adaptability is Key

- Digital marketing is dynamic. Be ready to tweak your goals based on evolving trends and insights.

Summary: Your Digital Marketing Roadmap

Setting realistic goals and objectives is like creating a roadmap for your digital marketing journey. It gives you direction, keeps you on track, and allows you to celebrate achievements along the way. Remember, each goal is a stepping stone toward your ultimate success in the digital realm.

In the next chapter, we'll delve into the essential skills every digital marketer should master. Get ready to elevate your digital marketing game!

CHAPTER 3: ESSENTIAL DIGITAL MARKETING SKILLS:

Section: Analytical Skills in Digital Marketing

Welcome to the fascinating world of Analytical Skills in Digital Marketing! As a beginner, you're about to uncover the power of numbers and data, turning them into your secret weapons for success.

Understanding Analytical Skills:

Digital marketing is more than just creating eye-catching content; it's about understanding how your efforts impact your audience and, ultimately, your business. Analytical skills involve the ability to collect, interpret, and draw meaningful insights from data.

Why Analytical Skills Matter:

Imagine having a treasure map but not knowing how to read it. Analytical skills are your decoding tool in the vast landscape of digital marketing. They help you:

Measure Success: Track and understand the performance of your campaigns.

Identify Trends: Spot emerging patterns in user behavior and market trends.

Optimize Strategies: Fine-tune your approach based on what's working and what's not.

Developing Analytical Skills:

For beginners, diving into analytics might seem overwhelming, but fear not! Here are some steps to help you develop your analytical prowess:

Learn the Basics: Familiarize yourself with key metrics like impressions, clicks, conversions, and bounce rates.

Explore Tools: Get hands-on experience with analytics tools such as Google Analytics, Facebook Insights, or SEO analytics platforms.

Interpret Data: Understand what the numbers are telling you. For instance, a high bounce rate might indicate that your landing page needs improvement.

Interactive Insights – Case Study:

Let's say you're running a social media campaign. By analyzing the data, you notice a spike in engagement after posting videos. This insight guides you to create more video content, capitalizing on what resonates with your audience.

Summary: Analytical skills are your compass in the digital marketing landscape. They empower you to make informed decisions, optimize your strategies, and achieve meaningful results. As you embark on your digital marketing journey, embrace the numbers, and let them guide you towards success!

In the next chapter, we'll explore the exciting realm of Creativity and Design in digital marketing. Get ready to unleash your artistic side while driving impactful campaigns!

Introduction:

Welcome to the exciting world of Creativity and Design in Digital Marketing! In this chapter, we'll explore how unleashing your creative side can elevate your digital marketing efforts. Whether you're a budding entrepreneur, a freelancer, or part of a marketing team, embracing creativity is key to making your mark in the digital landscape.

Section 1: The Power of Creativity:

What is Creativity in Digital Marketing?

Uncover the role creativity plays in capturing attention, building brand identity, and creating memorable campaigns.

Why Creativity Matters:

Explore how creative elements enhance user engagement, drive brand recall, and set your marketing efforts apart from the crowd.

Interactive Insight:

Creativity Exercise: Unlock Your Imagination

Engage readers with a simple creativity exercise. Encourage them to brainstorm and jot down creative ideas for a fictional digital marketing campaign. This hands-on activity sparks inspiration and emphasizes the importance of thinking outside the box.

Section 2: Design Basics for Beginners:

The ABCs of Design:

Break down design principles in a beginner-friendly manner. Cover topics such as color theory, typography, and layout to lay the foundation for effective visual communication.

Tools of the Trade:

Introduce easy-to-use design tools suitable for beginners. Mention platforms like Canva and Adobe Spark that empower even those with no formal design training to create stunning visuals.

Interactive Insight:

Design Challenge: Create Your First Visual Post

Provide step-by-step instructions for creating a simple visual post using a chosen design tool. This hands-on challenge boosts confidence and demonstrates the practical application of design principles.

Section 3: Telling Your Brand Story Through Design:

Understanding Branding:

Explore how design elements contribute to building a cohesive brand identity. Emphasize the importance of consistency across various digital channels.

Visual Storytelling:

Dive into the art of visual storytelling and how it captivates audiences. Showcase successful examples of brands effectively using visuals to convey their narrative.

Interactive Insight:

Brand Mood Board Activity

Encourage readers to create a mood board for their imaginary brand. This activity helps them translate their brand personality into visual elements, reinforcing the impact of design in storytelling.

Summary:

In this chapter, we've unlocked the door to creativity and design in digital marketing. We've learned how creativity enhances engagement, explored design basics, and discovered the art of visual storytelling. Remember, embracing creativity isn't just about making things look good; it's about forging a connection with your audience that lasts.

As you embark on your digital marketing journey, don't be afraid to experiment, try new things, and let your creativity shine. In the ever-evolving digital landscape, those who embrace creativity and design are the ones who stand out and make a lasting impression. Ready to unleash your creativity? Let's dive into the next chapter!

Section 1: Technical Proficiency in Digital Marketing

Welcome to the technical side of digital marketing! In this section, we'll delve into why technical proficiency is crucial and explore some key aspects that every beginner should grasp.

Why Technical Proficiency Matters

Digital marketing is not just about creativity; it's also about navigating the technical landscape. From understanding analytics tools to managing website platforms, technical skills are the backbone of successful campaigns. As a digital marketer, your ability to harness technology will set you apart.

Key Technical Components for Beginners

Website Basics: Navigating the Digital Space

Understanding Domains and Hosting

Basics of Content Management Systems (CMS)

Analytics and Insights: Decoding Data

Introduction to Google Analytics

Key Metrics to Monitor

SEO Essentials: Boosting Visibility

Basic Understanding of Search Engines

Importance of Keywords and Meta Tags

Social Media Tools: Managing Platforms Effectively

Social Media Scheduling Tools

Analytics on Social Media Platforms

Interactive Insight: Build Your First Google Analytics Report

Let's put your knowledge to the test! Create a basic Google Analytics report for a hypothetical website. Identify the number of visitors, popular pages, and the traffic source. This hands-on exercise will make the concepts more tangible.

Summary: Mastering the Tech Side

Technical proficiency might seem daunting at first, but it's like learning a new language – practice makes perfect. Embrace the tools available and explore their functionalities. As a digital marketer, your technical prowess will not only streamline your work but also open doors to deeper insights and innovation.

Remember, the digital marketing landscape is dynamic. Stay curious, keep experimenting, and you'll find yourself not just navigating the technical waters but surfing the waves of success!

Communication and Copywriting in Digital Marketing

Introduction: Unlocking the Power of Words

In the vast landscape of digital marketing, your ability to communicate effectively can make or break your campaigns. This chapter is your gateway to mastering the art of communication and copywriting – the secret sauce behind compelling content that captivates your audience.

Section 1: The Essence of Effective Communication

3.3 Understanding Your Audience

Before crafting any message, you must know who you're talking to. Learn to create buyer personas, detailed profiles of your ideal customers. Knowing their preferences, pain points, and aspirations will guide your communication strategy.

1.2 Clear and Concise Messaging

In the digital realm, attention spans are short. Learn to convey your message succinctly. Be clear about what you're offering and why it matters. Avoid jargon and unnecessary complexity.

1.3 Building a Brand Voice

Your brand should have a distinct personality in its communication. Whether it's friendly, professional, or quirky, consistency builds trust. Discover how to infuse your brand voice into every piece of content.

Section 2: The Art of Copywriting

2.1 What is Copywriting?

Copywriting is the art of writing text for advertising or other forms of marketing. Dive into the fundamentals of persuasive writing and learn how to craft messages that not only inform but also persuade your audience to take action.

2.2 Creating Compelling Headlines

The headline is your first impression. Explore techniques to create magnetic headlines that grab attention. A great headline sets the stage for the rest of your content.

2.3 Crafting Engaging Body Copy

Your main message needs to be as engaging as the headline.

Discover the power of storytelling, addressing pain points, and providing solutions. Learn to write content that resonates with your audience.

Interactive Exercise: Sharpen Your Skills

Exercise 1: Audience Persona Creation

Take a moment to create a detailed audience persona for your product or service. Identify demographics, interests, and challenges your audience faces.

Exercise 2: Write a Persuasive Headline

Craft a headline for your imaginary product. Experiment with different styles and see which one feels most compelling.

Exercise 3: Storytelling Challenge

Tell a short story related to your product or service. Focus on creating an emotional connection with your audience.

Summary: Mastering the Art of Words

In this chapter, you've laid the groundwork for effective communication and copywriting in digital marketing. You understand your audience, can craft compelling headlines, and weave engaging stories. These skills will be your guide as you venture into creating impactful digital marketing campaigns.

CHAPTER 4: CREATING A PERSONAL BRAND

Importance of Personal Branding in Digital Marketing:

Introduction: Unleashing the Power of Personal Branding

In the vast landscape of digital marketing, standing out is crucial. Your personal brand is the secret sauce that sets you apart from the crowd. In this chapter, we'll delve into the significance of personal branding and how it can elevate your digital marketing career to new heights.

Section 1: What is Personal Branding?

Personal branding is not just about logos and fancy graphics. It's about shaping the perception others have of you within your professional field. In the digital realm, your personal brand is the story you tell through your online presence, showcasing your skills, personality, and unique value.

Interactive Insight: Take a moment to reflect on your favorite digital marketers. What elements of their personal brand resonate with you?

Section 2: Why Personal Branding Matters in Digital Marketing

Subsection 2.1: Building Trust and Credibility

In a world bombarded with information, people turn to those

they trust. A strong personal brand builds credibility, establishing you as an authority in your niche. Clients and employers are more likely to choose someone they view as authentic and knowledgeable.

Interactive Insight: Share a personal anecdote about a brand or individual who gained your trust through their online presence.

Subsection 2.2: Creating a Memorable Impression

First impressions are lasting impressions, especially online. Your personal brand is your digital handshake. A well-crafted brand ensures that people remember you for the right reasons, increasing the likelihood of partnerships, collaborations, and job opportunities.

Interactive Insight: What elements of a digital marketer's personal brand do you find memorable?

Section 3: Building Your Personal Brand

Subsection 3.1: Define Your Unique Value Proposition (UVP)

Identify what makes you stand out. Is it your creativity, analytical skills, or a unique perspective? Your UVP forms the core of your personal brand.

Interactive Insight: List three qualities that make you unique as a digital marketer.

Subsection 3.2: Consistent Branding Across Platforms

Consistency is key. Your brand should be recognizable across various digital platforms. From your LinkedIn profile to your Twitter handle, maintaining a cohesive image reinforces your brand.

Interactive Insight: Check your social media profiles. Are they consistent in terms of visuals, tone, and messaging?

Section 4: Nurturing and Evolving Your Brand

Subsection 4.1: Engage with Your Audience

Building a personal brand isn't a one-way street. Actively engage with your audience through comments, shares, and discussions. This creates a community around your brand.

Interactive Insight: Respond to a comment or message from your audience. How does it feel to connect with your community?

Subsection 4.2: Adapt and Grow

Digital marketing is ever-evolving, and so should your brand. Stay updated on industry trends, adapt your brand accordingly, and showcase your ability to embrace change.

Summary: The Power of Personal Branding Unleashed

In this chapter, we explored the transformative impact of personal branding in digital marketing. From building trust and credibility to creating memorable impressions, your personal brand is the key to unlocking opportunities in the digital realm. Remember, your brand is not just what you say about yourself; it's what others say about you when you're not in the room. So, craft a brand that speaks volumes even in your absence.

Building an Online Presence

Introduction:

Welcome to the digital world, where your online presence is the key to unlocking endless opportunities in the realm of digital marketing. In this chapter, we'll delve into the importance of building a strong online presence, the foundational steps you need to take, and tips for maintaining a consistent and engaging digital footprint.

Section 1: Why Your Online Presence Matters

Insight: Your online presence is essentially your digital identity. It's how the world perceives you, and in the realm of digital marketing, first impressions are crucial. A robust online presence establishes credibility, trust, and authority – essential elements for success in the digital landscape.

Tips:

Define Your Brand Persona: Clearly articulate who you are, what you stand for, and how you want to be perceived online.

Consistency Across Platforms: Use the same profile picture, handle, and bio across all your social media accounts for a cohesive brand image.

Section 2: Foundational Steps to Establish Your Online Presence

Insight: Building an online presence is like constructing a digital home. You need a sturdy foundation before adding the finishing touches. Let's explore the fundamental steps to get started.

Tips:

Create a website: Your website is your digital headquarters. Ensure it's user-friendly, visually appealing, and provides essential information about you or your business.

Optimize for Search Engines: Implement basic SEO strategies to improve your website's visibility on search engines.

Section 3: Crafting Engaging Content

Insight: Content is the heartbeat of your online presence. It's how you communicate, connect, and captivate your audience. Let's uncover the art of creating compelling content.

Tips:

Understand Your Audience: Tailor your content to resonate with your target audience's needs and preferences.

Diversify Content Types: Experiment with a mix of text, images, videos, and infographics to keep your audience engaged.

Section 4: Interactive Strategies for Online Presence

Insight: The digital realm offers various interactive avenues to connect with your audience. Let's explore strategies that make your online presence dynamic and engaging.

Tips:

Live Video Sessions: Host live Q&A sessions, product launches, or behind-the-scenes glimpses to humanize your brand.

User-generated Content: Encourage your audience to create and share content related to your brand, fostering a sense of community.

Summary:

Building an online presence is a continuous journey, not a destination. It's about creating a digital ecosystem that reflects your values, engages your audience, and leaves a lasting impression. By following the foundational steps, crafting engaging content, and embracing interactive strategies, you're laying the groundwork for a vibrant and influential online presence.

Remember, in the dynamic world of digital marketing, adaptability is key. Stay authentic, stay connected, and watch your online presence flourish.

Establishing Authority in Your Niche

Introduction:

Building authority in your niche is crucial for success in digital marketing. As a beginner, you might wonder, "How can I stand out in a crowded online space?" This chapter will guide you through the steps to establish yourself as an authority figure, gaining trust and credibility in your chosen field.

Understanding Authority:

Authority in digital marketing means becoming a go-to source of valuable information. It's not just about what you say but how you say it and the expertise you bring to the table.

Insights:

- **Content Quality:** Consistently create high-quality content. Whether it's blog posts, videos, or social media updates, aim for content that educates, informs, and solves problems within your niche.

- **Consistency is Key:** Regularly share your knowledge. Consistency builds trust and helps you stay on top of your audience's minds.

- **Engage with Your Audience:** Respond to comments, participate in discussions, and ask questions. Engaging with your audience fosters a sense of community and positions you as an approachable expert.

Interactive Element:

Activity: Content Calendar Planning

Create a content calendar for the next month. Identify key topics within your niche and plan when you'll release content. This helps you stay consistent and provides a roadmap for your authority-building journey.

Easy-to-Grasp Tips:

1. **Start with What You Know:** Share your existing knowledge. You don't have to be an expert from day one; you're on a journey of growth.

2. **Be Authentic:** People connect with real stories. Share your experiences, successes, and even failures. Authenticity builds trust.

3. **Utilize Different Formats:** Experiment with various content formats, like blog posts, videos, podcasts, and infographics. Different people prefer different mediums.

Summary:

Establishing authority is about consistently delivering valuable content, engaging with your audience, and being authentic. Remember, it's a journey, not a race. Your authority will grow over time as you continue to learn, share, and connect with your audience.

CHAPTER 5
MASTERING SOCIAL MEDIA MARKETING

Introduction:

In the world of digital marketing, various platforms offer unique opportunities to reach and engage with your target audience. Understanding the strengths and characteristics of each platform is essential for crafting effective marketing strategies.

3. Facebook

Overview:

- **Audience:** 2.8 billion monthly active users.
- **Demographics:** Diverse age groups, especially popular among adults.
- **Content Format:** Text, images, videos, and live broadcasts.

Insights:

- **Engagement:** Encourage interaction through likes, comments, and shares.
- **Ads:** Robust advertising platform with detailed targeting options.
- **Groups:** Utilize communities to build a more personal connection.

Summary: Facebook is a versatile platform suitable for various content types, making it a cornerstone of social media marketing.

2. Instagram

Overview:

- **Audience:** 1 billion monthly active users.
- **Demographics:** Predominantly younger audience, visually-focused content.
- **Content Format:** Photos, videos, stories, and IGTV.

Insights:

- **Visual Storytelling:** Leverage the power of captivating visuals.
- **Hashtags:** Boost discoverability through strategic hashtag use.
- **Influencer Marketing:** Collaborate with influencers for wider reach.

Summary: Instagram is an image-centric platform, ideal for businesses with visually appealing products or services.

3. Twitter

Overview:

- **Audience:** 330 million monthly active users.
- **Demographics:** Popular among professionals, concise content.
- **Content Format:** Tweets limited to 280 characters, images, and short videos.

Insights:

- **Real-time Engagement:** Stay current and participate in trending conversations.
- **Hashtags:** Key for discovery and engagement.

- **Visuals and Multimedia:** Enhance tweets with images and videos.

Summary: Twitter is a real-time platform where brevity and trending topics play a crucial role.

3. LinkedIn

Overview:

- **Audience:** 774 million users.
- **Demographics:** Business and professional-focused audience.
- **Content Format:** Articles, professional updates, and multimedia.

Insights:

- **Professional Networking:** Connect with industry professionals.
- **Content Publishing:** Share informative articles and updates.
- **Company Pages:** Establish and showcase your brand professionally.

Summary: LinkedIn is the go-to platform for B2B marketing and establishing professional connections.

Interactive Element:

Try This: Choose one platform that aligns with your target audience and business goals. Create a sample post or ad that you could share on that platform, keeping in mind the unique characteristics discussed.

Content Strategy for Social Media

Introduction:

In the world of digital marketing, social media stands out as a dynamic and powerful channel for connecting with your audience. However, success on social media isn't just about posting random content. It requires a well-thought-out content strategy. In this chapter, we'll explore how to craft a compelling content strategy for social media, even if you're just starting out.

Understanding Your Audience:

Before you start creating content, it's crucial to understand your target audience. Who are they? What are their interests, challenges, and preferences? Utilize social media analytics tools to gather insights into your audience demographics and behavior.

Choosing the Right Platforms:

Not all social media platforms are created equal. Each has its own unique audience and content style. Consider your target audience and choose platforms that align with your brand and goals. For beginners, starting with platforms like Instagram, Facebook, or Twitter can be a good foundation.

Content Calendar and Consistency:

Consistency is key in social media. Create a content calendar to plan your posts in advance. This helps maintain a regular posting schedule and ensures a variety of content types. Your calendar should include a mix of promotional content, educational posts, and engaging visuals.

Diversifying Content Types:

Social media users engage with various types of content. Experiment with a mix of images, videos, infographics, and written posts. Visual content often grabs attention, so don't hesitate to use eye-catching graphics or short videos to convey your message.

Telling Your Brand Story:

Social media is an excellent platform to humanize your brand. Share behind-the-scenes glimpses, success stories, and the people behind your products or services. This helps build a connection with your audience and fosters trust.

Encouraging Interaction and Engagement:

Social media is a two-way street. Encourage your audience to engage with your content by asking questions, running polls, or hosting contests. Respond promptly to comments and messages. This interaction not only builds a community but also boosts your visibility on these platforms.

Measuring Success with Analytics:

Use analytics tools provided by social media platforms to measure the performance of your content. Track metrics such as reach, engagement, and click-through rates. Analyzing this data helps you understand what works best for your audience and refine your strategy accordingly.

Insight:

Remember, quality trumps quantity. It's not about how often you post but about the value your content provides. Social media is about building relationships, so focus on creating content that resonates with your audience and adds value to their lives.

Summary:

Crafting a successful content strategy for social media involves understanding your audience, choosing the right platforms, maintaining consistency, diversifying content types, telling your brand story, encouraging engagement, and measuring success. By following these steps and adapting as needed, you'll' be well on your way to building a strong presence on social media, even as a beginner.

Engaging with Your Audience

Introduction: Welcome to the exciting world of engaging with your audience in digital marketing! In this chapter, we'll explore why connecting with your audience is crucial, strategies to boost engagement, and how to create lasting relationships with your customers.

Section 1: Why Engagement Matters

- *Building Relationships:* Understand how engaging with your audience fosters trust and loyalty, turning one-time customers into brand advocates.

- *Boosting Brand Visibility:* Engaged audiences are more likely to share your content, expanding your reach and increasing brand awareness.

- *Feedback Loop:* Learn how engagement provides valuable feedback, helping you refine your strategies based on audience preferences and needs.

Section 2: Strategies for Engagement

- **1. Social Media Interaction:**
  - Utilize Platforms Effectively: Tailor your content for each platform (Facebook, Instagram, Twitter, etc.) to maximize engagement.
  - Respond Promptly: Acknowledge comments, answer questions, and engage in conversations to humanize your brand.

- **2. Compelling Content Creation:**
  - Storytelling Techniques: Learn to tell your brand's story in a captivating way that resonates with your audience.
  - Visual Appeal: Understand the impact of visuals, including images and videos, in capturing and retaining audience attention.

- **3. Contests and Giveaways:**
  - Interactive Campaigns: Explore the power of contests and giveaways to encourage participation and generate excitement.
  - User-Generated Content: Encourage your audience to create content related to your brand, fostering a sense of community.

- **4. Email Engagement:**
  - Personalized Communication: Implement

personalization in email campaigns to make your audience feel valued.

. Call-to-Action Optimization: Craft compelling CTAs that drive engagement and prompt desired actions from your audience.

Section 3: Tools and Metrics for Engagement

. *Analytics Tools:* Introduce beginner-friendly analytics tools to measure engagement, such as Google Analytics and social media insights.

. *Key Metrics:* Understand metrics like likes, shares, comments, click-through rates, and conversion rates to gauge the success of your engagement efforts.

Interactive Exercise: Let's create a sample social media post together! Craft a post that encourages engagement – perhaps by asking a question or running a poll. Share your creation in the comments or discuss it with a fellow learner to get feedback.

Summary: In this chapter, you've discovered the significance of engaging with your audience in digital marketing. From social media interactions to crafting compelling content and utilizing tools for measurement, you're' equipped with actionable strategies to boost engagement. Remember, the more you connect with your audience, the more memorable and impactful your brand becomes.

Next Steps: Experiment with the engagement strategies discussed in this chapter. Monitor the responses and interactions to refine your approach continuously. The journey to becoming a successful digital marketer begins with building meaningful connections!

CHAPTER 6: SEARCH ENGINE OPTIMIZATION (SEO)

Introduction: Unlocking the Power of Search Engines

Welcome to the world of SEO, the cornerstone of digital marketing success. In this chapter, we'll' demystify the basics of Search Engine Optimization (SEO), helping you understand its fundamental principles and empowering you to enhance your online presence.

Section 1: What is SEO? Imagine the internet as a vast library, and search engines as the librarians guiding users to the most relevant books. SEO, or Search Engine Optimization, is the process of making your website one of those sought-after books. It involves optimizing your online content so that search engines, like Google, can easily find, index, and rank it.

Interactive Insight: Think of SEO as the librarian's cataloging system. The better organized and relevant your book (website) is, the higher it appears in the library's'(search engine's' catalog.

Section 2: The Three Pillars of SEO

1.-Page SEO

> 3. Title Tags and Meta Descriptions: Crafting your digital book cover.
>
> . Heading Tags: Organizing your content like chapters.

- Keyword Optimization: Using relevant keywords naturally.

- Quality Content: Writing an engaging and informative book.

2. Off-Page SEO

- Backlinks: Other books referencing yours.

- Social Signals: Recommendations and discussions about your book.

- Brand Mentions: The library buzzing about your content.

3.Technical SEO

3. Site Structure: The layout and organization of your library.

- Mobile Optimization: Ensuring your book is accessible to everyone.

- Page Speed: How fast your readers can access your content.

Interactive Insight: Picture your website as a book. On-Page SEO is about the content and structure of the book itself. Off-Page SEO involves what others say about your book. Technical SEO is like maintaining the library—ensuring it's well-organized and accessible.

Section 3: Keyword Research and Implementation

Keyword Research

- Tools for Research: Understanding what readers are searching for.

- Long-Tail Keywords: Niche topics that your book covers.

- Competition Analysis: Checking out other books in your genre.

Keyword Implementation

- Title and Headers: Placing keywords strategically.
- Content: Integrating keywords naturally.
- URLs: Making sure your books address reflects its content.

Interactive Insight: Keywords are like the index words in your book. Imagine readers searching for specific words—those are your keywords.

Summary: Putting It All Together

In this chapter, you've' dipped your toes into the vast ocean of SEO. Remember, SEO is about making your digital book (website) both appealing to readers (users) and easy for librarians (search engines) to find. By mastering the art of SEO, you're' not just creating a website; you're' writing a bestseller that captivates both your audience and search engines alike. As you continue your digital marketing journey, keep refining your SEO strategies, and watch your online presence soar.

Interactive Task: Reflect on your website as a book. What elements need optimization, and how can you make it more captivating for both readers and search engines?

Congratulations! You've' just taken your first steps into the exciting world of SEO. Stay curious and stay tuned for more insights in the next chapters of your digital marketing adventure.

Keyword Research and Optimization

Introduction: Unlocking the Power of Keywords

Welcome to the heart of digital marketing - –here words become the bridge between businesses and their audience. In this chapter, we'll' demystify the art and science of Keyword Research and Optimization, a cornerstone of successful digital marketing strategies.

Section 1: Understanding Keywords

1.at are Keywords?

3.3 Keywords are the words and phrases people type into search engines when looking for information or solutions.

- Examples: "best digital cameras," "how to lose weight," "affordable web design services."

".2 Why Keywords Matter

- Keywords connect your content to the right audience.
- They form the basis of SEO, helping your content rank higher in search engine results.
- Proper keyword usage enhances the relevance of your content.

Section 2: Keyword Research

2.1 Getting Started with Research

- Tools for keyword research: Google Keyword Planner, SEMrush, Ahrefs.
- Understanding your target audience's language.

2.2 Long-tail Keywords

- Exploring the benefits of longer, more specific phrases.
- Lower competition and higher conversion rates.

2.3 Competitor Analysis

- Learning from competitors successes and failures.
- Identifying gaps and opportunities in your niche.

Section 3: Keyword Optimization

3.1 On-Page Optimization

- Placing keywords strategically in titles, headings, and throughout your content.
- Crafting compelling meta descriptions.

3.2 Quality Content and Keywords

- Writing for humans while keeping search engines in mind.

- Balancing keyword density for natural readability.

3.3 Mobile Optimization

- The importance of mobile-friendly content.

- Mobile search trends and adapting your keyword strategy.

Insights and Tips:

- **User Intent:**
    - Understanding the intent behind keywords for more targeted content.
    - Crafting content that directly addresses user queries.

- **Seasonal Keywords:**
    - Recognizing the impact of seasonality on search trends.
    - Adjusting your keyword strategy for timely relevance.

Interactive Activities:

- **Keyword Brainstorming:**
    - Encourage readers to brainstorm potential keywords for their business or content niche.
    - Provide a template for organizing and evaluating these keywords.

- **Competitor Keyword Hunt:**
    - Guide readers on how to analyze competitors for keywords.
    - Suggest a checklist for extracting valuable insights.

Summary: Unlocking Your Digital Potential

Mastering keyword research and optimization opens the door to a world where your content is not just seen but valued. Remember, keywords are the compass guiding your digital journey. The right ones will steer your content to the top, connecting your brand with those actively seeking what you offer.

In the next chapter, we'll' delve into the captivating realm of Content Marketing - –here your words don't 'just rank high; they resonate deeply.

On-Page and Off-Page SEO

Section 1: On-Page SEO

On-Page SEO is like the foundation of a building. It's 'what you control directly on your website.

1.optimizing Content

3.3 **Title Tags:** Craft compelling titles with relevant keywords.

- **Meta Descriptions:** Write concise and engaging meta descriptions.

- **Header Tags:** Use H1, H2, and H3 tags to structure content.

- **Keyword Placement:** Strategically place keywords in your content.

1.2 URL Structure

- **Short and Descriptive URLs:** Create URLs that give users an idea of the page content.

1.3 Image Optimization

- **Alt Text:** Describe images using alt text for search engines.

- **File Size:** Compress images for faster page loading.

1.4 User Experience (UX)

- **Mobile-Friendly Design:** Ensure your website is

accessible on mobile devices.

- **Page Speed:** Optimize loading times for a better user experience.

1.5 Technical SEO

- **Sitemap:** Create and submit a sitemap to search engines.

- **Robot.txt:** Control what search engines can and cannot index.

- **SSL Certificate:** Secure your website with HTTPS.

Interactive Tip: Use an SEO plugin like Yoast or All in One SEO for WordPress to guide you through On-Page SEO optimization.

Section 2: Off-Page SEO

Off-Page SEO involves activities outside your website that impact your site's 'visibility.

2.1 Link Building

- **Backlinks:** Acquire quality backlinks from reputable websites.

- **Anchor Text:** Use relevant anchor text for links.

2.2 Social Media Signals

- **Shareable Content:** Create content that people want to share.

- **Social Media Presence:** Maintain active profiles on relevant social platforms.

2.3 Online Reputation Management

- **Reviews and Ratings:** Encourage positive reviews and manage negative feedback.

- **Brand Mentions:** Monitor and respond to brand mentions online.

2.4 Influencer Marketing

- **Collaborate with Influencers:** Partner with influencers to expand your reach.

Interactive Tip: Explore tools like Moz or Ahrefs to track your backlinks and monitor your website's 'authority.

Summary:

- **On-Page SEO:** It's 'about optimizing your website's 'content, structure, and technical aspects for both users and search engines.

- **Off-Page SEO:** Focuses on building a reputable online presence through external factors like backlinks, social signals, and reputation management.

By mastering both On-Page and Off-Page SEO, you create a holistic strategy to boost your website's 'visibility and credibility on the internet.

CHAPTER 7: CONTENT MARKETING

Introduction: *Unveiling the Power of Content*

- Welcome to the World of Content Marketing
- Why Content is King in Digital Marketing

Section 1: Understanding Content Marketing

1.fining Content Marketing

3.3 What is Content Marketing?

- How Content Differs from Traditional Advertising

1.2 The Purpose of Content Marketing

- Building Trust and Credibility
- Establishing Thought Leadership
- Generating Leads and Conversions

Section 2: Core Components of Successful Content Marketing

2.1 Identifying Your Audience

- The Importance of Knowing Your Audience
- Creating Buyer Personas

2.2 Crafting Compelling Content

- Types of Content (Blog posts, Videos, Infographics, etc.)
- The Art of Storytelling in Content Creation

Interactive Element: Creative Exercise

- Develop Your Own Content Idea for a Hypothetical Business

2.3 Optimizing for Search Engines (SEO)

- Integrating Keywords Naturally
- Importance of High-Quality, Relevant Content

Interactive Element: SEO Checklist

- A Quick Guide to Optimize Your Content for Search Engines

Section 3: Content Distribution Strategies

3.1 Social Media and Content

- Choosing the Right Platforms
- Creating Shareable Content

Interactive Element: Social Media Content Calendar

- Plan Your Social Media Content for a Week

3.2 Email Marketing and Content

- Building an Email Subscriber List
- Crafting Engaging Email Content

Interactive Element: Email Content Template

- Design Your First Email Campaign

Section 4: Measuring Content Performance

4.1 Introduction to Analytics

- Key Metrics to Track (Views, Clicks, Conversions)
- Tools for Analyzing Content Performance

Interactive Element: Analytics Challenge

- Analyze a Sample Content Report and Answer Questions

Section 5: Tips for Beginners

5.1 Consistency is Key

- Establishing a Content Schedule
- Balancing Quality and Quantity

5.2 **Learning from Successful Content Marketers**

- Case Studies and Success Stories
- Emulating Best Practices

Conclusion: Your Journey Begins

- Recap of Key Concepts
- Encouragement to Begin Your Content Marketing Journey
- Resources for Further Learning

Summary: "Content Marketing Demystified keeps you on a journey into the heart of digital marketing's 'powerhouse content. From understanding the fundamentals to crafting compelling content and distributing it effectively, this chapter equips beginners with the essential knowledge. Engage in interactive exercises, create your content, and measure its success with practical tips. Your adventure in content marketing starts here!

Crafting Compelling Content

Introduction: Welcome to the heart of digital marketing - –rafting compelling content. In this chapter, we'll' delve into the art and science of creating content that captivates your audience, builds trust, and drives results.

Section 1: Understanding Your Audience: Before you start creating content, it's 'crucial to understand your audience. Who are they? What challenges do they face? What are their interests? We'll' guide you through the process of creating audience personas and tailoring your content to meet their needs.

Interactive Tip: Take a moment to create a simple persona for your target audience. What are their pain points? What solutions can your content offer?

Section 2: The Elements of Compelling Content: Learn the key elements that make content compelling. From attention-grabbing headlines to engaging storytelling, we'll' explore the components that keep your audience hooked.

Interactive Exercise: Write a catchy headline for a piece of content related to your chosen niche. Share it with a friend or colleague to get feedback.

Section 3: Visual Appeal and Multimedia: Discover the power of visuals in digital marketing. We'll' discuss the impact of images, videos, and infographics on audience engagement and provide tips on creating visually appealing content.

Interactive Tip: Experiment with creating a simple graphic or short video related to your content. Tools like Canva or Adobe Spark can make this process beginner-friendly.

Section 4: SEO-friendly Content: Understand the basics of Search Engine Optimization (SEO) and how it can elevate your content. Learn how to incorporate relevant keywords, optimize meta descriptions, and enhance your content's 'visibility on search engines.

Interactive Exercise: Identify a few keywords related to your content. Use them strategically in a short piece of writing and observe how it influences search engine results.

Section 5: Storytelling Techniques: Explore the power of storytelling in digital marketing. We'll' guide you through effective storytelling techniques that connect with your audience emotionally and make your content memorable.

Interactive Exercise: Share a personal or industry-related story that relates to your content. Encourage readers to share their stories in the comments.

Section 6: Building Trust Through Authenticity: Authenticity is the cornerstone of compelling content. Discover how to be genuine and transparent in your communication, fostering trust with your audience.

Interactive Tip: Share a behind-the-scenes glimpse of your work or a real-life experience related to your content. Ask your audience to share their authentic stories.

Summary: Crafting compelling content is an ongoing journey that involves understanding your audience, mastering various elements, and staying true to your authentic voice. By creating content that resonates, you'll' not only attract and retain your audience but also establish a lasting impact in the digital landscape.

Interactive Reflection: What key elements of compelling content resonate with you the most? How can you incorporate these into your own digital marketing efforts?

Content Distribution Strategies in Digital Marketing

Welcome to the world of Content Distribution! In this chapter, we'll' unravel the secrets behind getting your awesome content in front of the right audience. Remember, creating fantastic content is only half the battle; the other half is ensuring it reaches the people who need it. Let's 'dive in!

1.understanding Content Distribution:

3. **Insight:** Think of content distribution as the bridge connecting your content and your audience. It's 'the process of making sure your masterpiece doesn't 'sit in a digital attic but is actively discovered and consumed.

   . **Interactive Tip:** Imagine your content as a gift; distribution is the wrapping paper and the delivery service combined!

2. Leveraging Social Media:

   . **Insight:** Social media platforms are like bustling marketplaces. Don't 'just shout about your content;

engage with your audience, build relationships, and become a familiar face in the crowd.

- **Interactive Tip:** Pick a social platform you enjoy and explore how others in your niche share content. What catches your eye? Learn from the best!

3.O Magic for Visibility:

3. **Insight:** Search engines are like digital librarians. Make your content library easy to find by optimizing it for search engines through strategic use of keywords and relevant meta tags.

- **Interactive Tip:** Google your own content topic. What results grab your attention first? Analyze and incorporate similar elements in your strategy.

4.ail Marketing Delight:

3. **Insight:** Email is your direct line to your audience. Build a mailing list, and regularly share your content. Be personal, solve problems, and don't 'just sell.

- **Interactive Tip:** Craft an engaging email subject line. Pretend you have only five words to grab attention—what would you write?

5.Collaborate and Conquer:

3. **Insight:** Join forces with others in your field. Guest post on blogs, collaborate on podcasts, and share each other's 'content. It's 'a win-win!

- **Interactive Tip:** Reach out to someone in your niche for a collaboration. It could be as simple as sharing each other's 'content on social media.

6. Paid Promotion Precision:

- **Insight:** If your budget allows, consider paid advertising. Platforms like Google Ads and social media ads can give your content an extra push.

- **Interactive Tip:** Set a small budget for a social media ad campaign. Monitor the results and adjust your strategy based on what works.

Summary: Content distribution is the unsung hero of digital marketing. It transforms your content from a hidden gem to a shining beacon that attracts your target audience. Remember, it's 'not just about sharing; it's 'about engaging, optimizing, and building connections. Experiment with different strategies, track your results, and refine your approach as you go. Happy distributing!

Interactive Question for Readers: What content distribution strategy are you most excited to try, and why?

Measuring Content Performance in Digital Marketing

Introduction: Welcome to the world of content marketing! Creating compelling content is just one part of the equation; measuring its performance is equally crucial. In this chapter, we'll' dive into the tools and metrics that will help you gauge the effectiveness of your content marketing efforts.

Section 1: Setting the Stage for Measurement

- **Understanding Objectives:** Clearly define your content goals. Are you looking to increase brand awareness, drive traffic, or generate leads? Knowing your objectives sets the foundation for measurement.

- **Defining Key Performance Indicators (KPIs):** Identify KPIs relevant to your goals. Examples include website traffic, social shares, conversion rates, and engagement metrics.

Section 2: Tools for Measurement

- **Google Analytics:** Explore the basics of Google Analytics to track website traffic, user behavior, and content performance. Learn how to set up goals and measure conversions.

- **Social Media Insights:** Understand platform-specific analytics tools (e.g., Facebook Insights, Twitter Analytics) to assess social engagement, reach, and audience demographics.

- **Email Marketing Analytics:** Dive into metrics like open rates, click-through rates, and conversion rates to evaluate the impact of your email campaigns.

Section 3: Content-Specific Metrics

- **Page Views and Unique Visitors:** Measure the overall visibility of your content by tracking page views and unique visitors.

- **Time on Page:** Understand how long visitors are spending on your content. Higher time on page often indicates engaged readers.

- **Bounce Rate:** Evaluate the percentage of visitors who navigate away from your site after viewing only one page. A high bounce rate may suggest the need for content improvements.

- **Conversion Rates:** Measure how well your content converts visitors into leads or customers. This could be signing up for newsletters, downloading resources, or making a purchase.

Interactive Insight: Imagine you wrote a blog post and noticed a high bounce rate. What steps could you take to improve user engagement? Share your thoughts and strategies in the comments section below.

Section 4: A/B Testing for Content Optimization

- **What is A/B Testing:** Introduce the concept of A/B testing to compare two versions of content to see which performs better.

- **Testing Elements:** Discuss elements like headlines, CTAs, images, and even the content format. Encourage beginners to experiment and learn from the results.

Summary: Measuring content performance is about more than just numbers; it's 'about understanding audience behavior and optimizing your strategy. By setting clear objectives, using analytics tools, and focusing on content-specific metrics, you'll' gain valuable insights to refine your future efforts. Don't 'forget the power of A/B testing – it's 'your secret weapon for continuous improvement!

Remember, the key is not just to gather data but to use it strategically. As you embark on your content marketing journey, keep an eye on the metrics that align with your goals and be ready to adapt based on what the data tells you. Happy measuring!

CHAPTER 8: EMAIL MARKETING UNLOCKING THE POWER OF PERSONALIZED COMMUNICATION EMAIL MARKETING

Introduction: Welcome to the world of Email Marketing, a dynamic and essential component of digital marketing that enables direct communication with your audience. In this chapter, we'll' explore the basics of email marketing, its significance, and how you can leverage it to build lasting relationships with your audience.

Section 1: Understanding Email Marketing

- What is Email Marketing?
  - Definition and Purpose
  - Differentiating between Promotional and Transactional Emails
- Why Email Marketing Matters

- Building Trust and Credibility
- Direct and Personalized Communication
- Cost-Effective and High ROI

Section 2: Getting Started with Email Marketing

- Building Your Email List
  - Permission-based Marketing
  - Strategies for Growing Your Subscriber Base
- Choosing an Email Marketing Platform
  - Popular Platforms for Beginners
  - Understanding Features and Pricing

Section 3: Crafting Compelling Email Campaigns

- Segmentation and Personalization
  - Tailoring Content to Different Audiences
  - The Power of Personalized Subject Lines
- Designing Engaging Emails
  - Best Practices for Email Layout
  - Using Visuals and Multimedia

Section 4: Effective Email Copywriting

- Writing Irresistible Headlines
  - Grabbing Attention from the Start
  - A/B Testing for Optimal Results
- Creating Persuasive Body Content
  - Clear and Concise Messaging
  - Call-to-Action Optimization

Interactive Element: Try crafting a subject line or email content based on the tips provided. Share your creations in the community forum for feedback!

Section 5: Navigating Regulations and Best Practices

- Understanding CAN-SPAM and GDPR
  - Ensuring Compliance with Email Laws
  - Balancing Promotion with Privacy

- Frequency and Timing
  - Finding the Sweet Spot for Sending Emails
  - Analyzing Metrics for Optimization

Section 6: Analyzing Email Performance

- Metrics that Matter
  - Open Rates, Click-Through Rates, Conversion Rates, and more
  - Using Analytics Tools to Measure Success

Interactive Element*:* Set up an email campaign and analyze its performance using an email marketing platform. Share your insights and discuss strategies with fellow beginners.

Conclusion: Congratulations! You've' unlocked the potential of Email Marketing. It's 'not just about sending emails; it's 'about building connections, providing value, and achieving your marketing goals. As you embark on your journey, remember to stay creative, stay personal, and stay connected with your audience. Happy emailing!

Building and Nurturing an Email List

Introduction: The Power of Email Marketing

- Briefly explain why email marketing is a powerful tool in digital marketing.

- Highlight its cost-effectiveness, direct communication, and high conversion rates.

Section 1: The Foundation -Building Your Email List

Subsection 1.1: Creating Irresistible Lead Magnets

- Define what lead magnets are and why they are crucial.

- Examples of lead magnets: eBooks, cheat sheets, webinars, exclusive content.

- Tips for creating compelling lead magnets that resonate with your target audience.

Subsection 1.2: Optimizing Sign-Up Forms

- The importance of user-friendly sign-up forms.
- Placement, design, and simplicity of sign-up forms.
- A/B testing for optimal performance.

Subsection 1.3: Leveraging Social Media and Website Integration

- Strategies for promoting your email list on social media.
- Integrating sign-up forms seamlessly into your website.
- Using pop-ups effectively without annoying your audience.

Section 2: Nurturing Your Email List

Subsection 2.1: Crafting Engaging Welcome Emails

- The significance of the welcome email.
- Tips for creating a warm and engaging welcome sequence.
- Setting expectations for future communication.

Subsection 2.2: Designing Effective Email Campaigns

- Importance of segmentation for targeted campaigns.
- Crafting compelling subject lines and email content.
- Incorporating visuals and multimedia for better engagement.

Subsection 2.3: Building Trust Through Consistency

- The frequency of emails and finding the right balance.
- How to avoid spammy tactics and build trust.
- Encouraging two-way communication with your audience.

Interactive Element: Workshop Break

- Include an interactive exercise for readers to apply what

they've' learned so far.

- Task: Develop a lead magnet idea and design a corresponding sign-up form.

Insight: Personalization and Automation

- Emphasize the power of personalization in email marketing.
- Introduction to automation tools and their role in nurturing leads.

Summary: Key Takeaways

- The importance of a well-nurtured email list in digital marketing.
- Strategies for building and maintaining a quality email list.
- The role of personalization and automation in effective email campaigns.

Conclusion: Your Email Marketing Journey Begins

- Encourage readers to implement what they've' learned.
- Tease upcoming chapters that will delve into analytics and optimizing email campaigns.

Remember to keep the language simple, include visual aids, and encourage readers to apply the concepts immediately. This approach makes the content interactive and easy for beginners to grasp.

Email Marketing Crafting Effective Campaigns

Introduction: Welcome to the power-packed world of Email Marketing! In this chapter, we'll' delve into the art of crafting effective email campaigns. Email marketing remains a cornerstone in digital marketing, allowing direct communication with your audience. Let's 'explore how to make your emails stand out and achieve the desired results.

Section 1: Understanding Your Audience

- Know Your Subscribers:
    - Segment your audience based on demographics, behavior, or preferences.
    - Personalization - –he key to capturing attention.
- Crafting Relevant Content:
    - Tailor your message to suit the needs and interests of each segment.
    - Use engaging language that resonates with your audience.

Section 2: Designing Compelling Emails

- Eye-Catching Subject Lines:
    - The first impression matters create subject lines that spark curiosity.
    - Avoid spam-trigger words to ensure your emails land in the inbox.
- Responsive Design:
    - Optimize your emails for various devices (desktop, mobile, tablet).
    - Clear and visually appealing layouts enhance the user experience.
- Interactive Elements:
    - Incorporate buttons, quizzes, or surveys for engagement.
    - Encourage users to interact directly within the email.

Section 3: Call-to-Action (CTA) Strategies

- Clear and Compelling CTAs:
    - Craft actionable and concise CTAs.
    - Experiment with button colors and placement

for optimal results.

- Sense of Urgency:
    - Use words that prompt immediate action.
    - Limited-time offers or exclusive deals create urgency.
- Testing CTAs:
    - A/B test different CTAs to understand what resonates best.
    - Analyze data to refine and optimize future campaigns.

Section 4: Automating Email Sequences

- Welcome Emails:
    - Craft a warm and inviting welcome email for new subscribers.
    - Set expectations and introduce your brand's 'value.
- Drip Campaigns:
    - Nurture leads with a series of targeted emails.
    - Adjust content based on user interactions.
- Abandoned Cart Emails:
    - Remind customers about items left in their cart.
    - Incentivize with discounts or free shipping.

Interactive Insight:

Imagine you're' a subscriber receiving an email. What subject line would prompt you to open it? How can a CTA in an email encourage you to take action? Share your thoughts and ideas in the comments section.

Summary: Email marketing, when done right, is a powerful tool for building and maintaining relationships with your audience. Remember to understand your audience, design visually appealing emails, master the art of CTAs, and leverage automation for efficiency. Stay tuned for the next section where we explore the wonders of analytics in digital marketing!

Analytics and Optimization: Unleashing the Power of Data

Introduction Welcome to the data-driven world of digital marketing! In this chapter, we'll' demystify the magic behind analytics and optimization, empowering you to make informed decisions that drive success. So, grab your digital magnifying glass, and let's 'dive into the fascinating realm of numbers and insights.

Section 1: The ABCs of Analytics **1.1 Understanding Analytics**

- Definition: What Are Analytics in Digital Marketing?
- Types of Analytics: Web, Social Media, Email, and more.
- Tools of the Trade: Google Analytics, Facebook Insights, and others.

1.2 Setting Up Analytics

- Step-by-Step Guide: Installing Analytics on Your Website
- Key Metrics to Track: Visitors, Conversions, Bounce Rate, and more.
- Common Pitfalls: Avoiding Data Misinterpretation.

Section 2: Decoding the Data **2.1 Interpreting Analytics Data**

- Turning Numbers into Insights
- Identifying Trends and Patterns
- Recognizing Key Performance Indicators (KPIs)

2.2 Customer Journey Analysis

- Mapping the Customer's 'Digital Path

- Touchpoints and Conversion Funnels
- Recognizing Bottlenecks and Opportunities

Interactive Exercise

- Analyze your website's 'data using Google Analytics. Identify the top-performing pages and the ones that need improvement. What insights can you gather?

Section 3: Optimization Magic **3.1 The Art of Optimization**

- Definition and Importance in Digital Marketing
- Continuous Improvement Mindset
- A/B Testing: Experimenting for Success

3.2 Website Optimization

- Speed Matters: Importance of Page Load Time
- Responsive Design: Tailoring for Every Device
- Crafting Effective Call-to-Actions (CTAs)

3.3 Content Optimization

- Quality Over Quantity: Crafting Engaging Content
- SEO Basics: Enhancing Visibility
- Multimedia Magic: Adding Visual Appeal

Interactive Exercise

- Choose a webpage or social media post. Brainstorm and implement three optimization strategies. Monitor the analytics to see the impact.

Summary: Transforming Data into Dollars Congratulations! You've' just scratched the surface of the vast world of analytics and optimization. By understanding your data and continuously optimizing your digital presence, you're' not just a marketer; you're' a digital alchemist turning insights into success. Stay curious, keep experimenting, and watch your digital kingdom flourish!

CHAPTER 9: PAID ADVERTISING IN DIGITAL MARKETING: UNLOCKING GROWTH

Welcome to the exciting world of Paid Advertising, where your marketing efforts can directly translate into increased visibility and conversions. In this chapter, we'll' demystify the realm of Paid Advertising, exploring its significance, strategies, and how you can harness its power to elevate your digital marketing game.

Understanding Paid Advertising

Definition and Purpose

Paid Advertising involves paying for ad space to promote products or services on various digital platforms. The primary goal is to reach a specific audience and drive desired actions, such as clicks, conversions, or brand awareness.

Platforms Overview

- **Google Ads:** Dominating the search engine landscape, Google Ads allows you to bid on keywords to display your ads prominently in search results.

- **Facebook Ads:** With billions of active users, Facebook offers precise targeting options based on demographics, interests, and behaviors.

- **Instagram Ads:** Leverage the visual appeal of Instagram to showcase products or services through engaging visuals and stories.

- **LinkedIn Ads:** Ideal for B2B marketing, LinkedIn allows you to target professionals based on job titles, industries, and company sizes.

Crafting Effective Ad Campaigns

Identifying Objectives

Before diving into ad creation, define your goals. Are you looking to increase website traffic, generate leads, or boost sales? Clarifying objectives guides your entire campaign.

Target Audience

Understanding your audience is key. Define demographics, interests, and online behavior to tailor your ads to resonate with your target market.

Compelling Ad Copy and Design

- **Headline:** Craft a catchy headline that grabs attention.

- **Body Text:** Clearly communicate your value proposition and call-to-action.

- **Visuals:** Use eye-catching images or videos relevant to your message.

Budgeting and Bidding Strategies

Setting a Budget

Determine how much you're' willing to spend daily or over the campaign period. Start small and adjust based on performance.

Bidding

Understand the bidding system of the platform you're' using. Google Ads, for instance, employs a bidding system where you compete with others for ad placement.

Ad Performance Monitoring and Optimization

Analytics Tools

Leverage platform analytics and tools like Google Analytics to track the performance of your ads. Monitor metrics such as clicks, impressions, and conversion rates.

A/B Testing

Experiment with different ad variations to identify what resonates best with your audience. Test headlines, visuals, and calls-to-action.

Summary: Your Path to Success in Paid Advertising

Paid Advertising is a dynamic and powerful tool, but success requires a strategic approach. Begin by understanding your audience, setting clear goals, and crafting compelling ad content. Regularly monitor performance, tweak your strategy based on data, and stay adaptable.

Unlock the potential of Paid Advertising to propel your digital marketing efforts to new heights. Remember, experimentation and continuous learning are your allies in this ever-evolving landscape. Happy advertising!

Budgeting and Bidding Strategies in Digital Marketing

Welcome to the exciting world of budgeting and bidding in digital marketing! This chapter will guide you through the essentials of allocating your resources wisely and optimizing your bids for maximum impact.

1.understanding Budgeting in Digital Marketing

3. *Budgeting Basics:*

- Define Your Objectives: Clearly outline your marketing goals to allocate your budget effectively.

- Consider Your Costs: Factor in advertising costs, tools, and resources needed for campaigns.

- Start Small, Scale Gradually: Begin with a manageable

budget and increase as you gain insights and see results.

Budget Allocation:

- Prioritize Channels: Identify high-performing channels based on your target audience and goals.
- Testing Budget: Allocate a portion for experimenting with new strategies and channels.

2. Bidding Strategies for Success

Bidding Fundamentals:

- Cost Per Click (CPC): Pay for each click on your ad.
- Cost Per Mille (CPM): Pay for a thousand impressions.
- Cost Per Acquisition (CPA): Pay when a specific action is completed (e.g., a purchase or sign-up).

Bid Optimization Techniques:

- Manual Bidding: Set bids manually based on your analysis and strategy.
- Automatic Bidding: Let platforms adjust bids based on algorithms and user behavior.
- Bid Adjustments: Modify bids for specific demographics, devices, or locations.

3.Interactive Insights

3. *Scenario-Based Learning:*

- Explore hypothetical scenarios to understand how different bidding strategies affect outcomes.
- Q&A Sessions: Answer common questions about budgeting and bidding.

Interactive Exercises:

- Budgeting Simulation: Engage in a simulated budgeting exercise to make strategic decisions.

- Bid Optimization Challenge: Practice adjusting bids for better performance.

4.Summary and Takeaways

3. *Key Points Recap:*

- Clear Budgeting Objectives: Align your budget with specific marketing goals.

- Strategic Allocation: Prioritize channels and allocate resources accordingly.

- Bid Smartly: Choose bidding strategies based on your campaign objectives.

Insights for Success:

- Regular Monitoring: Keep an eye on campaign performance and adjust budgets as needed.

- Flexibility: Be willing to adapt your strategy based on real-time data and market trends.

Final Thoughts: Budgeting and bidding are dynamic aspects of digital marketing that require continuous refinement. Embrace a learning mindset, stay updated with industry changes, and don't 'be afraid to experiment.

Remember, the key to success lies in finding the right balance between budgeting wisely and optimizing bids strategically. As you delve into this chapter, approach it with curiosity and a willingness to learn – your journey to mastering digital marketing has just taken another exciting turn!

Ad Copywriting and Design

In the world of digital marketing, crafting compelling ad copy and designing eye-catching visuals is an art form that can significantly impact the success of your campaigns. In this chapter, we'll' delve into the fundamentals of ad copywriting and design, offering practical insights for beginners.

Section 1: The Power of Words - –d Copywriting

1.understanding Your Audience

3.3 Before you start writing, know your audience. What are their pain points, desires, and preferences? Tailor your language to resonate with them.

1.2 Crafting Attention-Grabbing Headlines

The headline is your first impression. Make it concise, impactful, and relevant to the user's 'search intent or interests.

1.3 Compelling Ad Descriptions

In the limited space available, create a compelling narrative. Highlight key benefits, use action-oriented language, and include a clear call-to-action (CTA).

1.4 A/B Testing and Iteration

Don't 'settle for your first draft. Conduct A/B tests with different ad copies to identify what resonates best with your audience. Continuously refine and iterate based on performance metrics.

Section 2: Visual Appeal - –d Design

2.1 Importance of Visual Elements

Humans are visual beings. The right design can capture attention, convey your message, and evoke emotions. Understand the psychology of colors, fonts, and imagery.

2.2 Consistency Across Platforms

Maintain a consistent visual identity across different platforms. This builds brand recognition and trust. Ensure your visuals align with your overall brand image.

2.3 Mobile-Friendly Designs

Given the rise of mobile users, optimize your ad designs for smaller screens. Ensure clarity, simplicity, and easy readability on various devices.

2.4 Incorporating High-Quality Imagery

Invest in high-quality images or graphics that align with your brand and message. Avoid clutter and ensure that visuals enhance, not distract from, your ad copy.

Section 3: Interactive Exercises

3.1 Headline Crafting Challenge

Engage readers with a hands-on exercise to create attention-grabbing headlines for different products or services. Encourage sharing results for feedback.

3.2 Design Mood Board

Guide readers to create a mood board representing their brand's 'visual identity. This helps in understanding the importance of consistency in design.

3.3 A/B Testing Simulation

Walk beginners through a simulated A/B testing scenario. Discuss the outcomes and emphasize the iterative nature of ad copy and design improvement.

Summary:

In the dynamic world of digital marketing, ad copywriting and design are pivotal. They shape the user's 'perception, influence click-through rates, and ultimately drive conversions. Understanding your audience, embracing creativity, and leveraging data-driven insights will empower you to create impactful ads that stand out in the crowded online landscape. As you embark on your digital marketing journey, remember: testing, learning, and adapting are your keys to success.

Chapter 10: Analytics and Data Interpretation in Digital Marketing

Analytics and the Pulse of Digital Marketing:

Welcome to the heartbeat of digital marketing - Analytics! In this chapter, we'll explore why understanding the numbers is key to steering your digital marketing ship towards success.

Why Analytics Matters:

Understanding the Audience: Analytics provides insights into who your audience is, where they come from, and what they do on your platforms. This knowledge helps you tailor your strategies to match their preferences and behaviors.

Measuring Effectiveness: Imagine running a race blindfolded; you might be moving, but you won't know if you're winning. Analytics acts as your vision, helping you track the performance of your campaigns, websites, and social media efforts. Are your efforts paying off? Analytics has the answer.

Data-Driven Decision Making: Analytics transforms guesswork into precision. By analyzing data, you can make informed decisions about where to allocate resources, what content to create, and how to optimize your campaigns for better results.

Diving into Analytics:

Understanding Key Metrics: Get acquainted with essential metrics like website traffic, conversion rates, click-through rates (CTR), and bounce rates. These numbers provide a snapshot of your digital marketing health.

Conversion Tracking: The crown jewel of analytics! Learn to set up conversion tracking to measure specific actions users take, be it making a purchase, signing up for a newsletter, or downloading a resource. This insight helps refine your strategies for maximum impact.

Social Media Analytics: Platforms like Facebook, Instagram, and Twitter offer detailed analytics. Explore engagement rates, reach, and demographics to fine-tune your social media content and engagement strategies.

Interpreting Analytics:

Identifying Trends: Analytics is your time machine. Spot trends over time - when are your audience most active? What content performs better during specific seasons? Use this knowledge for strategic planning.

Detecting Pitfalls: Analytics isn't just about celebrating victories; it's about learning from setbacks. Identify what didn't work, understand why, and use this information to tweak your approach for future success.

Summary:

In the vast ocean of digital marketing, analytics is your compass. It guides you, providing real-time feedback on what works and what doesn't. Embrace the data; let it be the wind in your sails. As you progress in your digital marketing journey, remember - analytics isn't just numbers; it's your key to unlocking the full potential of your efforts.

Interactive Insight:

Try accessing the analytics dashboard of your preferred social media platform or website. Look at the key metrics. What insights can you gather about your audience? What patterns or trends do you notice? This hands-on experience will make analytics less intimidating and more actionable.

Congratulations! You've just taken your first step into the fascinating world of digital marketing analytics.

Tools for Analytics in Digital Marketing:

Welcome to the world of digital marketing analytics! In this chapter, we'll explore the essential tools that empower marketers to measure, analyze, and enhance their strategies. Whether you're just starting out or looking to expand your knowledge, these tools will be your trusted companions on the journey to digital marketing success.

1. Google Analytics: Unveiling User Insights

Insight: Google Analytics is the powerhouse of web analytics. It provides a detailed overview of your website's performance, user behavior, and traffic sources. By diving into metrics like page views, bounce rates, and conversion rates, you gain a profound understanding of what resonates with your audience.

Interactive Tip: Set up your own Google Analytics account. Navigate through the dashboard and explore real-time data. Look for patterns and correlations in user behavior.

2. Facebook Insights: Navigating Social Engagement

Insight: For social media mavens, Facebook Insights is your go-to tool. It unveils valuable data about your audience's preferences, post reach, and engagement levels. Understand which content sparks interest and tailor your strategy accordingly.

Interactive Tip: Connect your Facebook Page to Insights. Explore the demographic data of your followers. Identify the top-performing posts and understand why they resonated.

3. Moz: Unraveling the World of SEO

Insight: Moz is a treasure trove for SEO enthusiasts. From keyword analysis to backlink tracking, it equips you with the insights needed to optimize your content for search engines. Uncover opportunities to improve your website's ranking and visibility.

Interactive Tip: Use Moz's Keyword Explorer. Find relevant keywords for your niche and analyze their search volume. Understand how to integrate these keywords organically into your content.

4. Mailchimp Analytics: Decoding Email Campaigns

Insight: Email marketing is a potent tool, and Mailchimp Analytics helps you harness its full potential. Track email open rates, click-through rates, and subscriber behavior. Identify trends and fine-tune your campaigns for maximum impact.

Interactive Tip: Create a sample email campaign using Mailchimp. Monitor its performance metrics, and experiment with different elements to see how they affect engagement.

5. SEMrush: Conquering Competitor Analysis

Insight: In the competitive landscape of digital marketing, knowing what your rivals are up to is crucial. SEMrush provides insights into your competitors' strategies, keywords, and backlinks, empowering you to refine your own approach.

Interactive Tip: Enter your website into SEMrush. Explore the organic search positions of your competitors. Identify gaps and opportunities to improve your own rankings.

Summary:

In the dynamic realm of digital marketing, analytics is your guiding light. These tools empower you to make informed decisions, refine your strategies, and ultimately drive success. As you embark on your digital marketing journey, remember that analytics isn't just about numbers; it's about understanding your audience and adapting to their evolving needs.

Takeaway: Embrace these tools as your allies. Regularly explore their features, experiment with different settings, and most importantly, use the insights gained to refine your digital marketing approach. The more you engage with these tools, the sharper your marketing acumen will become.

Remember, analytics isn't a one-time endeavor—it's an ongoing process of refinement and improvement. Happy analyzing!

Making Data-Driven Decisions in Digital Marketing:

Welcome to the exciting world of data-driven decision-making in digital marketing! In this chapter, we'll explore the power of data and how it can guide your marketing strategies for optimal success.

1. Understanding the Basics of Data-Driven Marketing

- **Why Data Matters:** Learn why data is the backbone of successful digital marketing campaigns. Understand how it provides insights into customer behavior, preferences, and the performance of your marketing efforts.

- **Key Metrics for Beginners:** Dive into fundamental metrics such as website traffic, conversion rates, click-through rates, and social media engagement. Understand what these metrics mean and how they impact your overall strategy.

2. Tools for Data Analysis

- **Introduction to Analytics Tools:** Explore popular analytics tools like Google Analytics. Learn how to navigate these platforms to gather meaningful data about your website, social media, and advertising performance.

- **Setting Up Tracking:** Step-by-step guide on setting up tracking codes and tags to monitor user interactions, conversions, and other essential events on your digital platforms.

3. Interpreting Data for Actionable Insights

- **Identifying Trends:** Discover how to spot trends and patterns in your data. Recognize the significance of sudden spikes or drops in metrics and understand what they might indicate.

- **Segmentation for Precision:** Learn the importance of segmenting your audience and campaign data. Tailor your marketing strategies based on the unique characteristics of different customer segments.

4. Using Data to Optimize Campaigns

- **A/B Testing:** Explore the concept of A/B testing and how it can help you refine your marketing messages, design elements, and calls-to-action for better performance.

- **Optimizing Ad Spend:** Understand how data can guide you in allocating your budget effectively. Identify which channels and campaigns are delivering the best return on investment.

Interactive Exercises:

- **Data Analysis Scenarios:** Present real-world scenarios and guide readers through the process of analyzing data. This hands-on approach helps beginners apply the concepts they've learned.

- **Case Studies:** Share success stories of businesses that transformed their strategies based on data insights. Break down these case studies to highlight key takeaways for your readers.

Summary:

Congratulations, you've completed the journey into the realm of making data-driven decisions in digital marketing! By embracing the power of data, you have the ability to fine-tune your campaigns, understand your audience better, and achieve marketing success with confidence.

Remember, data is not just numbers; it's your secret weapon for unlocking the full potential of your digital marketing efforts. As you continue your journey, always let the data be your guide, and watch your campaigns thrive in the ever-evolving digital landscape.

Chapter 11: Staying Updated and Adapting to Changes

Keeping Up with Industry Trends in Digital Marketing

Introduction: Welcome to the dynamic world of digital marketing, where staying ahead of the curve is the key to success. In this chapter, we'll explore the importance of keeping up with industry trends, how to do it effectively, and why it's crucial for your success as a digital marketer.

1. The Pace of Change: Digital marketing is ever-evolving, with new technologies, strategies, and platforms emerging constantly. Understanding the pace of change is the first step in realizing the need to stay informed.

Insight: The landscape can shift rapidly; what worked yesterday might not work tomorrow. Embracing change positions, you as an adaptable and forward-thinking marketer.

2. Why Keeping Up Matters: Staying current with industry trends isn't just about following the crowd. It's about maintaining relevance, delivering value to your audience, and optimizing your strategies for better results.

Insight: Trends shape consumer behavior, and being ahead allows you to anticipate needs, tailor campaigns, and provide a seamless user experience.

3. How to Keep Up:

a. **Follow Industry Influencers:** - Identify and follow thought leaders and influencers in digital marketing. - Engage with their content, participate in discussions, and learn from their experiences.

SQL Copy code

Insight: Connecting with influencers not only provides insights but also expands your professional network.

b. **Attend Webinars and Conferences:** - Participate in webinars, virtual conferences, and industry events. - Engage in Q&A sessions and network with fellow attendees.

Arduino Copy code

Insight: Virtual events make industry knowledge accessible from the comfort of your home.

c. **Read Blogs and Newsletters:** - Subscribe to reputable blogs and newsletters focused on digital marketing. - Set aside time regularly to consume the latest articles and updates.

SQL Copy code

Insight: Bite-sized information from newsletters keeps you informed without overwhelming you.

d. **Join Online Communities:** - Become part of digital marketing communities on platforms like LinkedIn, Reddit, or industry-specific forums. - Participate in discussions, share your experiences, and ask questions.

sqlCopy code

Insight: Communities provide real-time insights, practical tips, and a support system for your journey.

4. Summary: Keeping up with industry trends is not a chore; it's a strategic move that sets you up for success. Embrace change, learn from experts, attend events, read voraciously, and engage with your community. In this ever-evolving field, your commitment to staying informed will be your greatest asset.

Interactive Element: Trend Tracker Exercise: Encourage readers to create a simple "Trend Tracker" document. List current trends, update it regularly, and jot down thoughts on how each trend could impact their digital marketing efforts. This hands-on approach makes learning about trends practical and actionable.

Continuous Learning and Professional Development in Digital Marketing:

Introduction: Unlocking Your Potential

- Welcome to the World of Lifelong Learning
- Why Continuous Learning Matters in Digital Marketing

1. The Rapidly Evolving Landscape of Digital Marketing

- The Ever-changing Digital Ecosystem
- Adapt or Lag Behind: Embracing Change in Digital Marketing
- Staying Ahead in a Dynamic Industry

Interactive Insight:

- **Activity:** Create a list of three recent changes or trends in digital marketing and brainstorm how they might impact your strategy.

2. Building Your Learning Toolbox

- Online Courses and Certifications
- Webinars and Workshops
- Industry Conferences and Events

Interactive Insight:

- **Self-Assessment:** Identify one area in digital marketing where you feel less confident. Research and list three courses or resources that could help you improve in that area.

3. Leveraging Digital Marketing Communities

- Joining Online Forums and Groups
- Networking on Social Media Platforms
- Learning from Industry Experts

Interactive Insight:

- **Discussion Starter:** Share your thoughts on a recent digital marketing trend in a relevant online community and engage in discussions with peers.

4. Embracing Mentorship and Networking

- Finding a Mentor in the Industry

- Networking Events and Meetups
- Peer-to-Peer Learning

Interactive Insight:

- **Networking Challenge:** Attend a local or online networking event, introduce yourself to at least two people, and discuss a recent digital marketing success or challenge.

5. Practical Application: The Power of Side Projects

- Starting a Blog or Personal Project
- Creating and Managing Social Media Campaigns
- Experimenting with New Tools and Technologies

Interactive Insight:

- **Mini-Project:** Start a small personal project related to digital marketing (e.g., a blog, Instagram account). Document your progress and share insights with your learning community.

Summary: Unleashing Your Potential

- Continuous Learning as a Mindset, not a Task
- The Symbiotic Relationship Between Theory and Practice
- Becoming an Agile and Adaptable Digital Marketer

Final Interactive Thought:

- **Personal Growth Pledge:** Write down one specific action you commit to taking in the next month to enhance your digital marketing skills. Share it in your learning community for mutual encouragement.

Conclusion: Your Digital Marketing Journey Unfolds

- Reflecting on Your Learning Path

- Excitement for the Ongoing Adventure
- Cheers to Your Continuous Growth in Digital Marketing!

Adapting to Algorithm Changes in Digital Marketing:

Introduction: Welcome to the dynamic world of digital marketing, where change is constant, and adaptation is key. In this chapter, we'll explore the importance of staying ahead of algorithm changes, understanding their impact, and implementing strategies to navigate through them.

1. The Dynamic Landscape: Digital marketing platforms, such as search engines and social media, constantly update their algorithms. These changes affect how content is ranked, displayed, and discovered. Understanding this dynamic landscape is crucial for digital marketers.

2. Monitoring Algorithm Updates: Stay informed about algorithm updates from major platforms like Google, Facebook, and Instagram. Follow official channels, blogs, and industry experts to receive timely information. Being proactive allows you to anticipate changes and adjust your strategies accordingly.

Interactive Tip: Set up Google Alerts for key terms like "digital marketing algorithm updates" to receive instant notifications.

3. Impact on Search Engine Optimization (SEO): Search engines frequently refine their algorithms to enhance user experience. Learn how algorithm changes influence SEO factors, such as keyword rankings, page speed, and mobile-friendliness. Adapt your SEO strategies to align with the latest guidelines.

Interactive Insight: Use online tools like Google's Page Speed Insights to assess and improve your website's performance.

4. Social Media Algorithm Shifts: Platforms like Facebook and Instagram regularly tweak their algorithms to prioritize content. Understand how these changes affect organic reach, engagement, and the visibility of your posts. Adjust your content strategy to align with the current algorithms.

Interactive Tip: Experiment with different types of posts and analyze engagement metrics to understand what resonates with your audience.

5. Data-Driven Decision Making: Utilize analytics tools to monitor the performance of your digital marketing efforts. Track key metrics, such as website traffic, click-through rates, and conversion rates. Analyzing data helps you identify the impact of algorithm changes and make informed decisions.

Interactive Insight: Explore Google Analytics to visualize and interpret data trends. Take advantage of free online courses to enhance your analytical skills.

6. Agility and Flexibility: Develop an agile mindset to adapt swiftly to algorithmic shifts. Being flexible allows you to experiment with new strategies, optimize campaigns, and capitalize on emerging trends. Embrace change as an opportunity for growth rather than a hurdle.

Interactive Tip: Create a "Testing Calendar" to schedule regular experiments with different ad creatives, keywords, or posting times.

Summary: Adapting to algorithm changes in digital marketing is not just a necessity; it's a skill that sets successful marketers apart. Stay informed, monitor performance metrics, and be ready to pivot your strategies. Remember, the ability to adapt is your secret weapon in the ever-evolving landscape of digital marketing.

Interactive Challenge: Share your insights or questions in our online community or social media groups. Engage with fellow marketers to gain different perspectives and stay updated.

Chapter 12: Building a Career in Digital Marketing

Introduction: Welcome to the exciting world of digital marketing careers! In this chapter, we'll explore the diverse job opportunities available in digital marketing and provide insights to help you find the perfect fit for your skills and interests.

1. Digital Marketing Generalist: *Insight:* Digital Marketing Generalists are versatile professionals who have a broad understanding of various digital marketing channels. They are responsible for creating and implementing comprehensive marketing strategies.

Interactive Tip: Discover your favorite digital marketing channels by experimenting with different platforms. Your passion will guide your specialization.

2. Social Media Manager: *Insight:* Social Media Managers focus on building and maintaining a brand's presence on social platforms. They create engaging content, interact with the audience, and analyze social media metrics.

Interactive Tip: Craft a social media strategy for a hypothetical business. Experiment with content creation and scheduling tools to get hands-on experience.

3. SEO Specialist: *Insight:* SEO Specialists optimize websites to rank higher on search engines. They conduct keyword research, improve website structure, and analyze data to enhance organic visibility.

Interactive Tip: Choose a niche and optimize a blog post for a specific keyword. Track its performance using Google Analytics and SEO tools.

4. Content Marketer: *Insight:* Content Marketers focus on creating valuable and relevant content to attract and retain a target audience. They often collaborate with SEO specialists to enhance content visibility.

Interactive Tip: Develop a content calendar for a month. Experiment with different types of content, such as blog posts, infographics, and videos.

5. Email Marketing Specialist: *Insight:* Email Marketing Specialists design and implement email campaigns to nurture leads and engage customers. They analyze data to optimize email performance.

Interactive Tip: Create a simple email campaign using a platform like Mailchimp. Monitor open rates and click-through rates to understand user engagement.

6. Paid Advertising Specialist: *Insight:* Paid Advertising Specialists manage and optimize online advertising campaigns. They work with platforms like Google Ads and Facebook Ads to reach specific target audiences.

Interactive Tip: Set up a small paid advertising campaign for a product or service. Monitor the results and adjust your strategy based on performance data.

Summary: Digital marketing offers a wide array of job opportunities, each catering to different skills and interests. Whether you prefer a holistic approach or want to specialize in a specific channel, there's a role for you. Experimenting with various aspects of digital marketing will not only help you discover your passion but also build a versatile skill set. The key is to stay curious, adapt to industry changes, and embrace the dynamic nature of digital marketing. Your journey in this ever-evolving field is just beginning!

Remember, the digital marketing landscape is vast, and your journey is uniquely yours. Enjoy the process of learning, experimenting, and carving your path in the exciting world of digital marketing.

Building a Career in Digital Marketing:

Section 1: Understanding Your Career Path

1.1 Freelancing in Digital Marketing

Overview: Freelancing in digital marketing offers flexibility and autonomy. As a freelancer, you have the freedom to choose your projects, clients, and working hours.

Insight: Pros:

- Flexibility and Work-Life Balance
- Diverse Range of Projects
- Direct Client Interaction

Cons:

- Inconsistent Income
- Self-Marketing Required
- Responsibility for Business Operations

Interactive Element: Explore a day in the life of a digital marketing freelancer through a fictional scenario. What challenges might they face, and how do they overcome them?

1.2 In-House Digital Marketing Roles

Overview: Working in-house means being employed by a single company to handle its digital marketing efforts. This offers stability and the chance to specialize in a particular industry.

Insight: Pros:

- Stable Income and Benefits
- Deep Industry Knowledge
- Team Collaboration

Cons:

- Limited Diversity in Projects
- Corporate Hierarchy
- Less Flexibility

Interactive Element: Create a checklist for someone considering an in-house digital marketing role. What key skills should they possess, and what questions should they ask during a job interview?

1.3 Digital Marketing Agencies

Overview: Agencies provide a dynamic environment with exposure to various clients and industries. This option allows you to work on different projects and collaborate with diverse teams.

Insight: Pros:

- Exposure to Varied Projects
- Collaborative Team Environment
- Professional Growth Opportunities

Cons:

- High Pressure and Deadlines
- Limited Control Over Client Selection
- Potential for Long Working Hours

Interactive Element: Present a virtual tour of a digital marketing agency, showcasing the different departments and roles. Allow readers to explore the agency environment through clickable elements.

Section 2: Making Informed Choices

2.1 Self-Reflection Exercise

Interactive Element: Include a self-assessment quiz to help readers identify their preferred work style. Based on their answers, guide them toward freelancing, in-house roles, or agency work.

2.2 Real-Life Stories

Insight: Share success stories and challenges from professionals in each career path. Highlight how individuals navigated their digital marketing careers, providing relatable experiences for beginners.

Interactive Element: Incorporate a forum or discussion platform where readers can share their thoughts, ask questions, and learn from each other's experiences.

Summary: Choosing the right career path in digital marketing involves a balance of personal preferences, skills, and professional goals. Whether you prefer the autonomy of freelancing, the stability of an in-house role, or the dynamic environment of an agency, the key is aligning your choice with your values and aspirations.

Networking and Building Professional Relationships in Digital Marketing:

Introduction

- Highlight the importance of networking in the digital marketing industry.
- Emphasize the role of professional relationships in career growth.
- Set the stage for beginner-friendly insights and interactive strategies.

Section 1: Why Networking Matters in Digital Marketing

Insight 1: Collaboration and Learning Opportunities

- Illustrate how networking opens doors to collaborative projects.
- Share anecdotes of successful partnerships in the digital marketing realm.
- Highlight the value of learning from peers and industry experts.

Insight 2: Job Opportunities and Career Advancement

- Explore how networking can lead to job opportunities.

- Discuss career advancements made possible through professional connections.
- Showcase stories of individuals who leveraged their network for success.

Section 2: Building Meaningful Connections

Insight 3: Authenticity and Personal Branding

- Stress the importance of being authentic in networking.
- Guide beginners on showcasing their unique skills and personality.
- Share examples of successful digital marketers who built strong personal brands.

Insight 4: Utilizing Social Media for Networking

- Provide tips on using social media platforms for professional connections.
- Recommend joining industry-specific groups and participating in discussions.
- Offer strategies for initiating conversations and building relationships online.

Section 3: Networking Events and Conferences

Insight 5: Attend Local and Virtual Events

- Encourage attendance at local meetups, workshops, and virtual conferences.
- Explain the benefits of face-to-face interactions in a digital world.
- Suggest platforms and websites to discover relevant events.

Insight 6: Effective Networking at Events

- Provide tips on approaching people at events.

- Share advice on exchanging contact information and following up.
- Include insights on making a lasting impression during networking events.

Section 4: Leveraging LinkedIn for Professional Growth

Insight 7: Optimizing Your LinkedIn Profile

- Guide beginners in creating a compelling LinkedIn profile.
- Emphasize the importance of a professional and engaging bio.
- Provide examples of well-crafted LinkedIn profiles in the digital marketing field.

Insight 8: Engaging with Your LinkedIn Network

- Encourage regular engagement with connections through comments and shares.
- Discuss the value of sharing insights, articles, and success stories.
- Highlight the potential for job opportunities and collaborations on LinkedIn.

Summary and Interactive Exercise

- Summarize key takeaways from the chapter.
- Include an interactive exercise where readers can practice networking skills.
- Provide a template for an "elevator pitch" that readers can customize for networking events.

Conclusion

- Reinforce the idea that networking is an ongoing process.
- Encourage readers to be proactive in building and

maintaining professional relationships.

. Express optimism about the exciting opportunities that networking can bring to a career in digital marketing.

Conclusion: Navigating Your Digital Marketing Odyssey

Congratulations, intrepid digital marketer! You've embarked on a journey that's as thrilling as it is rewarding. As we reach the final chapter of this guide, let's take a moment to reflect on the vast digital landscape you've explored and the skills you've honed along the way.

A Recap of Your Digital Expedition:

1. **Understanding the Digital Ecosystem:** We delved into the dynamic world of digital marketing, uncovering its diverse channels, from the ever-scrolling realms of social media to the intricate algorithms of search engines.

2. **Building a Sturdy Foundation:** Armed with knowledge, you fortified your understanding of your audience and set sail with purpose, anchoring your aspirations with realistic goals and objectives.

3. **Mastering Crucial Skills:** Your toolkit expanded to encompass not just technical prowess, but also the artistry of creativity, the precision of analytics, and the finesse of communication.

4. **Crafting Your Digital Persona:** You harnessed the power of personal branding, creating a beacon that illuminates your expertise and establishes you as a trusted navigator in your chosen niche.

5. **Sailing the Social Media Seas:** Navigating the vastness of social media, you learned to harness its waves, shaping engaging content that not only floats but sails smoothly in the turbulent currents.

6. **Unveiling the Secrets of SEO:** With a compass calibrated to the intricacies of SEO, you discovered the magic of keywords, the

dance of on-page and off-page optimization, and the science of ranking high in digital landscapes.

7. Crafting Compelling Content: In the ever-evolving world of content, you mastered the art of storytelling, creating narratives that resonate with your audience and leave an indelible mark.

8. Email Marketing: You built bridges with your audience through the ancient yet powerful channel of email, creating campaigns that not only land in inboxes but resonate with hearts and minds.

9. The Art of Paid Advertising: Venturing into the paid realms, you learned to strategically deploy your resources, creating advertisements that aren't just seen but leave an indelible impression.

10. Navigating Analytics Waters: Armed with a telescope pointed at data constellations, you deciphered the language of analytics, making informed decisions that propel your ship forward.

The Treasure Map for the Future:

As you stand on the deck of your digital vessel, poised for the future, remember that the map is ever-changing. Stay curious, adapt to the winds of change, and continue honing your skills. Your journey has only just begun.

An Interactive Challenge:

Before we part ways, here's a challenge for you: Take a moment to jot down three action items inspired by this guide. What will you implement first? Share your thoughts in the digital logbook of your choice, whether it's a physical notebook or your preferred digital platform.

Farewell and Bon Voyage:

As you set sail into the vast seas of digital marketing, remember: Every click, every engagement, and every conversion is a milestone in your journey. Embrace the challenges, celebrate the victories, and keep sailing towards your digital dreams.

Bon voyage, brave digital marketer. May your campaigns be

ever-clickable, your content ever-sharable, and your career ever-ascendant! Until we meet again on the shores of success.